Other Books by Jean Fritz

AND THEN WHAT HAPPENED, PAUL REVERE?
CAN'T YOU MAKE THEM BEHAVE,
   KING GEORGE?
GEORGE WASHINGTON'S BREAKFAST
SHH! WE'RE WRITING THE CONSTITUTION
WHAT'S THE BIG IDEA, BEN FRANKLIN?
WHERE DO YOU THINK YOU'RE GOING,
   CHRISTOPHER COLUMBUS?
WHERE WAS PATRICK HENRY ON THE
   29TH OF MAY?
WHY DON'T YOU GET A HORSE, SAM ADAMS?
WILL YOU SIGN HERE, JOHN HANCOCK?

JEAN FRITZ

Where do you think you're going, Christopher Columbus?

PICTURES BY MARGOT TOMES

PAPERSTAR

G. P. Putnam's Sons

The Putnam & Grosset Group

Library of Congress Cataloging-in-Publication Data
Fritz, Jean Where do you think you're going, Christopher Columbus?
Summary: Discusses the voyages of Christopher Columbus who determined
to beat everyone in the race to the Indies. 1. Colombo, Cristoforo—Juvenile
literature. 2. America—Discovery and exploration—Spanish—Juvenile literature.
3. Explorers—Spain—Biography—Juvenile literature. 4. Explorers—
America—Biography—Juvenile literature. [1. Columbus, Christopher.
2. Explorers. 3. America—Discovery and exploration—Spanish] I. Tomes, Margot.
II. Title. E111.F79 1980 970.01'5 [B] [920] 80-11377
ISBN 0-399-20723-6 (hardcover)
13 15 17 19 20 18 16 14 12
PaperStar ISBN 0-698-11580-5 (paperback)
3 5 7 9 10 8 6 4

To Michael—*Adelante!*

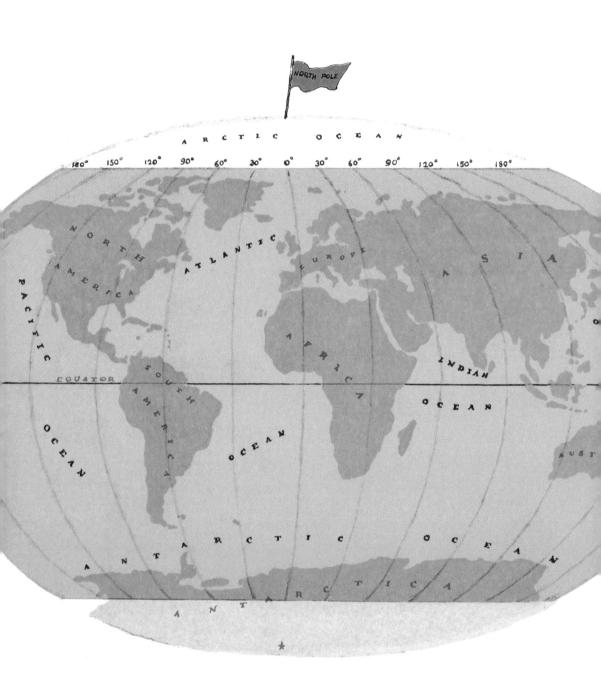

The world as it is

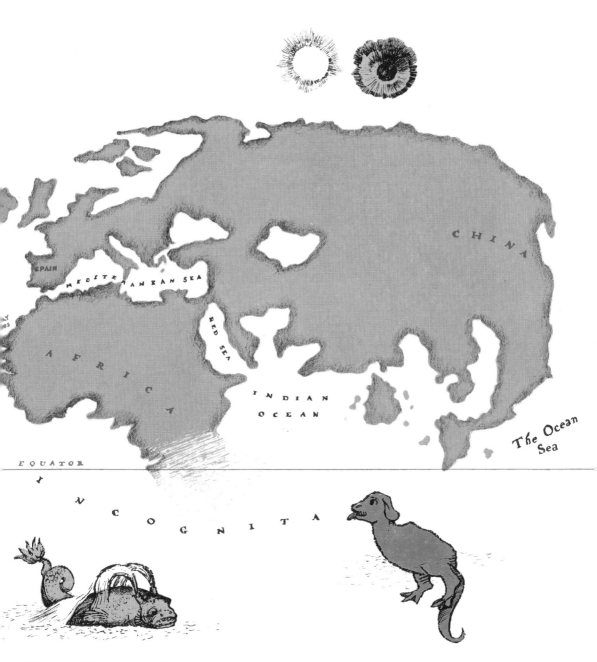

The world as Columbus imagined it

It was lucky that Christopher Columbus was born where he was or he might never have gone to sea. The city of Genoa sat smack on the west coast of Italy with the sea right outside its front door. Its harbors rocked with ships; its sailors sailed wherever men dared to sail. Of course some people (like Christopher's father, a master weaver) were content to stay in Genoa all their lives. But not Christopher Columbus. Whenever he had a chance, off he'd sail, his red stocking cap pulled down over his red hair, his gray eyes squinting to see all that he could see. Sailing, he said, made a person "wish to learn the secrets of the world."

And in 1451, when Columbus was born, there were still many secrets. Most people agreed that the world was round like a ball, but they didn't agree on how big the world was or how wide the ocean. Still, they did know that far away in the east there was a fabulous place called the Indies, which was overflowing with gold and jewels and spices. They had even bought these treasures from merchants who traded with other merchants in a long overland trail that stretched over thousands of miles of mountains and deserts. Then, in 1453, when Christopher Columbus was two years old, the merchants suddenly had to stop trading. The Turks, who had been fighting the Christians for centuries, put an end to overland travel, so now there'd be no more gold or spices unless someone could figure out another way of getting to the Indies.

Portugal was the country where people were figuring the hardest. So, of course, that was a good place for anyone interested in learning the secrets of the world. Christopher Columbus got there by accident. In 1476, when he was twenty-five years old, he was sailing past Portugal on a trading trip when all at once his ship was attacked by an enemy. He was wounded. Then he was flung into the sea, six miles from shore. His ship went down in flames; his friends drowned. Christopher Columbus would have drowned too except that he was lucky. He grabbed an oar floating by and slowly kicked his way to shore.

And there he was in Portugal. And there he stayed, off and on for nine years, running a store that sold maps, making trips to faraway places, listening to talk about the world's

secrets. He stayed until he had learned what he thought he needed to know and until he had decided what he wanted to do.

He was going to beat everyone in the race to the Indies. The king of Portugal was going about it the wrong way, he decided. The king was instructing his ships to sail around Africa and then head east, but his ships kept turning back. Oh, it was too far, the sailors moaned, and it was too scary. No one had ever sailed so far south. No one knew where Africa ended.

Columbus thought all this was a big waste of time. Why not take a short cut? Why not sail *west* to the Indies? Straight across the Ocean Sea.

Why not? Well, there were plenty of people to tell him why not. The Ocean Sea was no short cut, they said; it was a big place. It would take three years to cross it. You would run out of food and water. And how would you get back? Not with the wind. It didn't blow that way, people said. Even if it did, how could it blow you uphill? And it would have to. The world was round, wasn't it? Downhill, one way; uphill, the other. People laughed. That Christopher Columbus had some crazy ideas! If God had wanted His Ocean Sea crossed, He would have seen to it long ago. Not now. Not so late in the world's history.

But Columbus read books and found a few that agreed with him. (If they didn't agree, he stopped reading.) One writer said that a man could walk around the whole world in four years, sixteen weeks, and two days. Since Columbus was only going to the Indies and wouldn't be walking, he figured he didn't have far to go at all. Indeed, it was a "small sea" between Spain and India, according to an ancient Greek philosopher. This seemed reasonable to Columbus. How could nature be so unorderly, he asked, as to have more water than land? Dr. Toscanelli, a famous Italian scholar, estimated that there were only 3000 nautical miles between the Canary Islands (southwest of Portugal) and Japan. And Japan was the place in the Indies where Columbus most wanted to go.

Columbus had read all about the Indies in a well-known travel book written by Marco Polo, who had gone there on the overland route about two hundred years before. His stories about the riches and splendor of the Great Khan's court in China were so fantastic that he was accused of exaggerating. But Columbus believed him. Especially when he talked about the island of Japan (or Cipangu, as he called it) which supposedly had so much gold that whole palaces were built of it.

Japan was one of 7,448 islands in the Indies, Marco Polo said. An English travel writer, Sir John Mandeville, also wrote about the islands of the Indies. He claimed to have seen men with umbrella feet, people whose eyes were on their shoulders, griffons (half-lion, half-eagles), and ants that dug for gold. Actually, Mandeville was an out-and-out faker who had never been near the Indies, but many people (including Columbus) accepted his stories. Why wouldn't unknown parts of the world contain unknown forms of life?

So Columbus read, but it was not just books that finally convinced him. He believed that God Himself had revealed the secrets of the world to him. Indeed, God had arranged his life so that *he* would be the one to find the way to the Indies by sea. Nothing had been an accident. Not his birthplace, not his shipwreck, not even his name. In Latin the name Christopher means "Christ-bearing," and so obviously he was meant to take the Christian religion across the Ocean Sea and convert the people there. God had even arranged a useful marriage for him. In 1478, two years after he had landed in Portugal, he had married a young lady who came from a noble family with friends at court. So now Christo-

pher Columbus was not just a common seaman. There was nothing to stop him from going to the king of Portugal and asking for ships and money for his trip to the Indies.

In 1484 that is just what he did. Columbus was thirty-three years old now, a tall-standing, well-built man with ruddy cheeks and hair that was turning gray. He was too proud to be "soft of speech," as he, himself, admitted, so when he spoke to King John of Portugal, he spoke right out. He didn't *believe* he'd find the way to the Indies by going west; he *knew* he would. He didn't *hope* to bring back gold; he *promised* to bring it back.

In the end the king decided that Christopher Columbus was just a big talker and his counselors agreed. So King John told Columbus, No, thank you; the Portuguese would stick to the African route. And that was that.

John II · King of Portugal

The next year Columbus went to Spain. His wife had died, leaving him with a son, Diego, whom he put in the care of monks in a Spanish monastery. Then he went to see King Ferdinand and Queen Isabella. He was particularly hopeful that the queen would help him. After all, she was such an enthusiastic Christian that she insisted everyone in Spain be a Christian too. At the moment she was fighting a war with the Moors of southern Spain, who had the bad luck to be Mohammedans; later she would banish Jews from the country. Indeed, she was so religious that if she even found Christians who were not sincere Christians, she had them burned at the stake. (Choir boys sang during the burning so Isabella wouldn't have to hear the screams.) So, of course, Columbus was hopeful. The queen was one person who should understand that crossing the Ocean Sea to the Indies was not only the way to make Spain richer, but the way to turn more people into Christians.

The trouble was that Queen Isabella was too busy to think about the Indies. It was a year before Columbus could even see her, and then she didn't say yes. But she didn't say no either. She told Columbus to wait. So he waited. Week after week. Month after month. The longer he waited, the bigger he talked, until people began laughing and making jokes about him. Naturally this made Columbus mad, and when he got mad, he got red in the face and he said, "By San Fernando!" (He never swore.)

After two years of waiting, he was very red in the face and he decided, by San Fernando, he'd go back to Portugal! Maybe he could change King John's mind. But in Portugal everyone was celebrating the return of Bartholomew Diaz from Africa. He'd sailed all the way down the African coast and clear around the cape at the southern end. With such good news, King John couldn't bother with the silly schemes of Christopher Columbus.

Columbus returned to Spain. It was 1489 now and he had three more years to wait until the queen finished her war and beat the Moors. Only then did she think about the Indies. Only then did she finally say yes. She would help Columbus.

Pleased as he was, Columbus couldn't forget the wasted years and the jokes. He was forty-one years old now and he decided the queen would have to pay well for his services. He wasn't going to give away the riches of the Indies for nothing. He stated his terms. If he was successful, he must be knighted. He must be given the title of Admiral of the Ocean Sea, made viceroy and governor-general of all the lands he discovered, and granted one-tenth of the treasure brought back to Spain. Furthermore, these rights were to be passed down in his family.

The queen could hardly believe it. Who did Columbus think he was? If he was going to be so high and mighty, she said, he could just forget the whole thing. She was through with him.

But she wasn't through. At the very last minute the queen changed her mind. Columbus was already on his way to see the king of France when the queen called him back. She didn't want the king of France to get those riches. She would accept the terms, she said. After all, what could she lose? If Columbus didn't succeed, he'd get nothing. If he did succeed, let him have his terms; it would be worth it. So the contract was signed. All Columbus had to do now was to succeed.

At eight o'clock on the morning of August 3, 1492, Columbus set sail from Spain. He had three ships, the *Niña*, the *Pinta*, and the *Santa Maria* (on which he sailed), approximately 100 men, a company of cats to take care of rats that were always on shipboard, and an interpreter to speak to the people of the Indies. (The interpreter spoke Arabic, but this was such a foreign-sounding language that Europeans expected all foreigners to understand it.) As for supplies, Columbus took food (sea biscuits, salt meat, cheese, raisins, beans, honey, rice, almonds, sardines, anchovies), water, wine, firewood, compasses, and half-hour glasses. (A ship's boy kept track of the time by turning the glass every half hour to let the sand trickle the other way.) He took cannons, crossbows, and muskets in case the natives of strange islands were unfriendly, and in case they were friendly, he had a large stock of bells, scissors, knives, coins, beads, needles, pins, and mirrors to exchange for gold or any other treasure that was handy.

Eventually, of course, Columbus expected to meet with kings, so it was only proper that he carry letters of greeting from his own king and queen. One letter, written in Latin, was addressed to the Great Khan, the king of China. In fact, there hadn't been a Great Khan for 124 years, but no one in Europe knew that. Another letter was to Prester John, a rich Christian king who, according to Sir John Mandeville and others, was supposed to rule a wonderful country some-

where near the Indies. In fact, there was no Prester John and never had been. But no one could say that Columbus was not well prepared.

Certainly he was happy to be on his way, the sea rolling under him and the wind at his back. The ships stopped at the Canary Islands for last-minute repairs and supplies; then on September 6 they pulled up anchor and sailed into the Unknown.

"Adelante! Forward!" Columbus cried. The directions were simple: 2400 miles due west to Japan. (He had dropped 600 miles from Dr. Toscanelli's estimate.) The sailors knew, of course, that 2400 miles meant many days without sight of land, but they hadn't known how it would feel to have that vast circle of empty ocean settle around them for so long. Day after day the same circle, no matter how far or fast they sailed. And they were sailing fast—once 170 nautical miles in one day. Still, the circle didn't change. Or the wind either. It always blew in the same direction, taking them farther and farther west.

Yet if the sameness of the sea and the wind was scary, it was also scary to remember that they were in the Unknown, where anything might happen at any time. When a meteor with a long, branching tail of white fire streaked into the sea one night, they were terrified. Oh, it was a bad sign, the sailors cried. They should have stayed home.

And what did the captain-general, Christopher Columbus, say? "Adelante!" was what he said. It was all he ever said. When the sea turned into a meadow of green and yellow floating weeds, he said it. "Adelante!"—right through the weeds. When the wind dropped so that they could scarcely move, it was "Adelante" again. When they had sailed beyond the point where Japan was supposed to be, he repeated, "Adelante!"

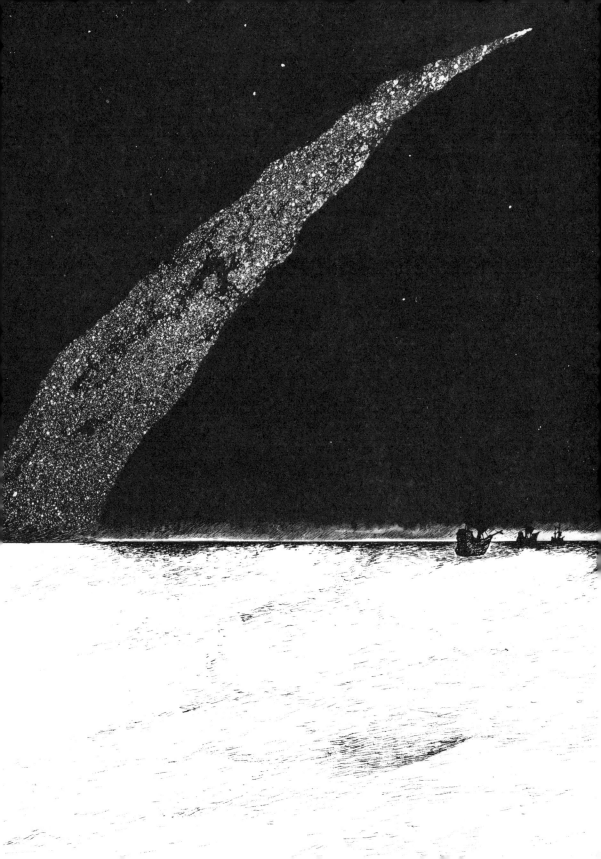

It was too much. Some of the sailors decided that they were being led to their death by a crazy man. Why, Columbus didn't even know enough to be afraid! He was actually enjoying this trip, talking about how soft the air was, how pleasant the mornings. At night he would stare at the sky for hours at a time as if he were reading a love story that he couldn't put down. More than once the sailors thought how easy it would be to push Columbus overboard some night when he was standing on deck "drunk with the stars."

But Columbus had ways to quiet the men. For one thing, he never let them know his actual reckoning of the distance covered each day. He pretended that they had not gone as far as he thought they really had so the voyage would not seem as long and "the people would not be frightened." Moreover, he kept pointing out encouraging signs that land was near. A live crab in the weeds. A whale. (Columbus supposed that whales stay near land.) One day they saw four land birds together. A great sign, Columbus said. *Four* birds wouldn't be lost. One day it rained—a drizzling rain. Land rain, Columbus said. Just like at home.

At sunset on September 25 Martin Pinzón, captain of the *Pinta*, shouted, "Tierra! Tierra! Land! Land!" Men clambered up the rigging of all three ships for a better view. Yes, it was land, all right. Glory be to God! At last, at last. Martin Pinzón was especially grateful. The person who sighted land first had been promised a handsome reward by the king and queen.

On September 26 there was no sign of land anywhere. They must have seen clouds on the horizon that looked like land.

On October 7 the *Niña* raised a flag and fired a cannon, the signal that land had been sighted. Another false alarm. Maybe they'd never find land, the men grumbled. Maybe there was no land in the west.

On October 10 the men announced that they could stand it no longer. They must turn back.

Well, of course, they should have known what Columbus would say, and, of course, he said it. "Adelante!" There was no use complaining, he told them. He had come to find the Indies and, by San Fernando, he'd find them! Three days, he said. Give him three days and they'd have land.

The next night Columbus gave orders that instead of dropping anchor, the three ships would sail right on. But look sharp, he said. And to the first man who sighted land, he promised a silk doublet or jacket in addition to the royal reward.

Columbus watched as eagerly as everyone else. At ten o'clock he noticed a light, like a little wax candle, wavering on the horizon. He couldn't be sure so he asked a servant standing nearby. Yes, the servant said, there did seem to be a light, but then it disappeared and Columbus put it out of his mind.

At two o'clock in the morning a cannon was fired from the *Pinta*. A young seaman named Rodrigo had seen white sand cliffs looming up in the moonlight. This time there was no doubt. They had been at sea thirty-seven days (since leaving the Canary Islands) and at last they had reached land. The three ships lay to, and with the first light of morning, everyone rejoiced to see a large, level island, "so green," Columbus said, it was a "pleasure to gaze upon."

For Columbus, it was a triumph—solid proof that he'd been right all along. Here he was in the Indies, fulfilling a plan that God had worked out for him step by step. When Rodrigo claimed the silk doublet and the royal reward, Columbus said no, he had, himself, sighted land when he'd seen a light at ten o'clock. How could it be otherwise? Surely God, who had gone to so much trouble to bring him here, meant him to have the honor. Certainly everyone else wanted to honor him. As soon as he had gone ashore and taken official possession of the island, the men crowded about Columbus, congratulating him, calling him admiral, governor-general, viceroy, and begging his forgiveness for their moments of doubt. All but Rodrigo. (He was so mad at Columbus that the first chance he got, he went to Africa and became a Mohammedan.)

Columbus named the island San Salvador. Certainly it wasn't Japan. There were no palaces and the only sign of gold was the gold rings that the natives wore in their noses. Indeed, that was all they wore. The people were as naked, Columbus said, "as their mothers bore them" which, of course, was pretty naked. Otherwise, they were normal-looking. They didn't have umbrella feet or eyes on their shoulders.

But if the Spaniards were surprised to see naked natives, the natives were even more surprised to see dressed Spaniards. All that cloth over their bodies! What were they

trying to hide? Tails, perhaps? The natives pinched the Spaniards to see if they were real and agreed that, pale as they were, they were flesh and bone. But where had they come from? There were no such people in the world they knew; they must have dropped down from the sky. So they gave the sky-people what gifts they had: cotton thread, darts, and parrots. In return, they received glass beads and tiny bells that went "chuque-chuque" when they were shaken.

What Columbus wanted, however, was information. Where was Japan? The interpreter stepped forward and spoke in Arabic, but he might as well have been talking to birds. No one understood. So Columbus tried sign language. He pointed to the gold nose rings and made motions that were supposed to mean, where? Where had the gold come from? The natives were very obliging. They pointed and made gestures too. Indeed, whatever the Spaniards did, the natives tried to copy. They would make good servants, Columbus said, for they were so willing. And good Christians too, for already they were crossing themselves like old-timers. But they were no help in giving directions. And in order to be a success in the eyes of the queen, Columbus had to find Japan. So it was up anchor and away again. Off to Japan, wherever that was.

In a way it was too bad that Columbus needed to find gold. He had such a good time that fall—sailing from island to island naming them all, planting crosses as he went, marveling at what he saw. Trees so tall they scraped the sky! Fish of all colors! Flocks of parrots that blotted out the sun! Flowers, fruit, birds—oh, it would take a thousand tongues to tell it all, he said, and then who would believe without seeing for himself?

And the curiosities! There were dogs that didn't bark. (A type of yellow hound that grunted instead of barking.) There were hanging beds (hammocks), mermaids (which were really sea cows), canoes that held forty men and more. And a leaf that men rolled up and, with one end lighted, stuck the other end up their nose and puffed (tobacco). He saw no human monstrosities in his travels, but he heard about them. From natives whom he'd taken aboard at San Salvador and taught a little Spanish, he was told of an island where men had dogs' heads; another where they had only one eye. Didn't this sound just like the stories that Sir John Mandeville told?

But Columbus wasn't finding Japan. Still, he knew that he had not been brought here for nothing, and when his native interpreters mentioned a place called Colba, he thought, aha, this was it! Colba must be Cipangu (Japan), only the natives were not pronouncing it right. Actually they were referring to the island which we now call Cuba, and even Columbus could see when he got there that it wasn't Japan. It didn't even look like an island and there wasn't a gold palace in sight.

Columbus made new calculations of his position and decided that this was China. "It is certain," he wrote, "that this is the mainland." Moreover, when he pointed toward the interior, the natives cried, "Cubanacan!" What else could that mean but "People of the Great Khan"? So Columbus told his Arabic interpreter to put on his best clothes; he was to lead a delegation to the court of the Great Khan and deliver the letter from the king and queen. A native guide would show him the way.

Six days later the delegation returned. All they had found was a village of fifty thatched huts and 1000 naked people. This was Cubanacan. (In fact, the word meant mid-Cuba.)

If Columbus was disappointed, he didn't show it in the day-by-day report that he wrote for the king and queen. He had only praise for his Indies and pointed out that it was so healthy that no one had even had a headache. But when it came to praying, Columbus prayed for gold. For five weeks he sailed along the coast of what he insisted was the mainland of China, hunting for gold. But what did he get? Parrots. Wherever he stopped, the natives gave him parrots.

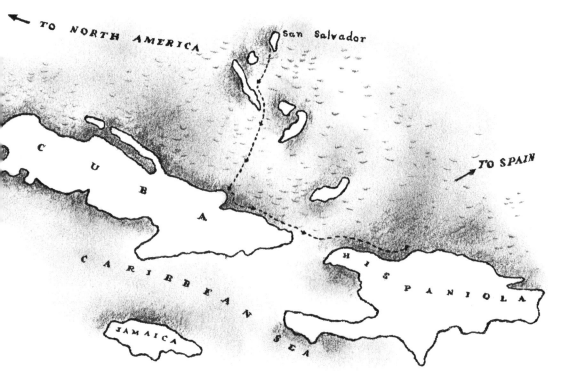

In December Columbus sailed to Haiti, which reminded him so much of Spain that he named it La Española (or Hispaniola as it came to be called—Spanish Island). The songbirds sang like Spanish songbirds here, the crickets chirped like Spanish crickets, and the fish (sole, mullet, lobsters) tasted like Spanish fish. Only there was more of everything and it was better. Indeed, Columbus ran out of adjectives to describe this island. If he told the whole truth, he said, he would be accused of exaggerating, like Marco Polo.

Best of all, there was gold. Not a lot, but some. Small chunks which the natives gave the Spaniards along with parrots and bread. Once a chief presented Columbus with two pieces of hammered gold. Columbus was so excited that he gave the chief the string of amber beads he was wearing, a pair of red shoes, and a bottle of orange water. Encouraging as this was, however, Columbus knew there wasn't nearly

enough gold to satisfy a queen. He had to find the gold mine that this gold had come from.

Meanwhile he was enjoying the natives, the friendliest he had met in all his travels. Night and day they came to the ships—men, women, and children, some swimming, some in canoes. On December 23, Columbus estimated that in the course of one hour more than 1000 persons visited the ships.

Among the visitors this week were messengers from a nearby king who invited Columbus to visit him. As a gift, the messengers brought a belt, four fingers wide, embroidered with red and white fishbones. The centerpiece was a mask with ears, nose, and tongue of hammered gold. The king had much gold, the messengers said, even banners of gold, for he lived near the source. Cipangu. The messengers didn't *say*

Cipangu, Columbus admitted in his report; they *said* Cybao (a region in central Hispaniola), but surely they meant Cipangu. So on December 24, Christopher Columbus, Admiral of the Ocean Sea, sailed north for the harbor closest to that part of Hispaniola that was obviously Japan.

Columbus and his crew had been so busy entertaining natives that they'd had no sleep for forty-eight hours, so, of course, by the evening of the twenty-fourth they were worn out. Columbus went to bed at eleven o'clock and the others followed, all but the helmsman who was steering and the little ship's boy who was turning the half-hour glass. But the helmsman was as sleepy as everyone else, and, rules or no rules, he handed over the tiller to the ship's boy. Nothing could happen on such a smooth sea, he assured the boy. And for one hour nothing did happen; then smoothly and quietly the ship went aground on a coral reef.

The boy gave the alarm and pell-mell the entire crew turned out. Above the uproar Columbus shouted orders and, by San Fernando, they all stepped lively that night! Still, no matter what they did, they couldn't get the ship off the reef. When it began to leak and tilt on its side, Columbus knew it was the end of the *Santa Maria*. In order to save the property on board, he would need many men and many canoes.

Columbus sent to the friendly king for help and by sunrise not only the king but hundreds of his subjects were on hand. All day they worked without stopping for even "a morsel of bread," Columbus reported, and when they had finished, there was nothing left on board and nothing lost, not even a nail.

While the men worked, the king tried to comfort Columbus. He hung a plate of gold around Columbus' neck, but Columbus was so upset that he needed a lot of comforting. The king gave him more gold; in return Columbus gave the king a shirt and a pair of gloves. Well, the king put on the gloves and was so pleased with himself that he gave Columbus a gold mask. They continued to comfort and appreciate each other until Columbus had collected a nice assortment of gold pieces and the king had added a scarlet coat, a silver ring, and colored boots to his wardrobe.

By this time Columbus saw that the loss of the *Santa Maria* was no tragedy after all. It was a good thing. Another of God's miracles. Columbus would go back to Spain, leaving some of his men on the island to gather gold. Then he would return with more and better ships to collect the gold that the men would have dug from the gold mine and the spices they would have gathered in Japan. In this way his return was ensured. Marveling at how cleverly God was taking care of him, Columbus ordered a fort to be built for the thirty-nine men he was leaving behind. And on January 4, 1493, he set sail for Spain.

For two weeks the *Niña* (with Columbus aboard) and the *Pinta* wound among the islands, stopping here and there to take on parrots and give away bells. When at last they struck open sea, the men were delighted to see how well they sailed uphill, if that's what they were doing. But then they ran into bad weather. "The ocean made up something terrible," Columbus wrote in his report, "and the waves crossed each other." The *Niña* and the *Pinta* were separated, each afraid that the other had gone down. Never had Columbus been more in need of a miracle and never had he prayed as hard. Everyone else prayed too. They would do anything, anything, they promised, if the Lord would only save them. They'd walk barefoot to church! They'd strip down to their shirts! They'd light five-pound candles! But

what if they weren't saved? Columbus worried that no one would ever know that he'd found the Indies, so he wrote it all down on a piece of parchment. He wrapped the parchment in cloth, covered it with a cake of wax, put it in a barrel, and threw the barrel overboard.

The barrel disappeared, but luckily it didn't matter. After six days the *Niña* limped into a harbor of a Portuguese island. True to their promise, the men took off their shoes and socks and trousers and marched off to church. And what happened? They were arrested. Not because of their dress (men often dressed this way to show that they were sorry for their sins) but because they were Spaniards. The Portuguese had no love for Spaniards.

Columbus explained that he was Admiral of the Ocean Sea and viceroy of the Indies, but the Portuguese were not impressed. Columbus said that he knew the king of Portugal personally. The king was far away, the Portuguese pointed out. Then Columbus stopped arguing. He wanted his men free, he shouted, and by San Fernando, they better be set free. Pronto!

Grudgingly the Portuguese gave in. The men returned to the ship, put on their trousers, shoes, and socks, and as soon as the water had calmed, they set off again. They had one more storm to ride out, and, on March 15, seven-and-a-half months after they'd left home, they arrived back in Spain. At the last minute the long-lost *Pinta* appeared and followed the *Niña* into port.

The news spread quickly. Remember the fellow who was going to the Indies? Well, he'd found them and now he was home. All across Spain people poured out to see Columbus and his strange procession making their way to the court at Barcelona. Columbus, richly dressed and ornamented, led the parade on horseback. He was followed by six natives (Indians, they were called now) wearing aprons, gold noseplugs, beads, and bracelets. Then came men carrying treasures from the Indies: cages of parrots, baskets of curiosities (plants, shells, native darts, thread), and, most important, samples of gold.

Columbus' big day of triumph came when he reached court. King Ferdinand and Queen Isabella didn't just sit still on their thrones, the way they usually did when people called. No, indeed. The king and queen stood to greet their admiral; then they invited him to sit beside them while he told his story. All the jokers who had laughed at Columbus in the past, all the doubters and the know-it-alls had to show him respect now, no matter how big he talked. For six weeks

Columbus remained at court, basking in glory. When the king went for a ride, he invited Columbus to come along and ride at his side. Before Columbus ate, a taster tasted the food from each of his dishes to make sure it wasn't poisoned, just as if he were a member of the royal family. He was given his own company of footmen to open doors for him and to serve him at table.

The queen was full of compliments. Columbus had shown more wisdom, she said, than could ever be expected of a mortal being, and Columbus had to agree. What he'd done, he admitted, was a miracle. His whole life had been a series of miracles and he had faith that the miracles would go on. After all, he had been *chosen* to do what he was doing. Perhaps because of this faith he began signing his name in a secret code that took the form of a pyramid.

.S.

.S. A.S.

X M y

.Xρο ΓΕΡΕΝS.

No one has ever known what the letters mean except for the last line, which is a Greek and Latin form of "Christopher," or "Christ-bearing." It was clear, however, that this mysterious signature not only had a religious meaning for him but also spelled success.

He could not know that he was then at the peak of his success. Nothing would ever be as good for him again.

In September 1493, Columbus set out on his second trip to the Indies, pennants flying, trumpets sounding, flutes playing, and cannon saluting on all sides. He had seventeen ships this time, 1,200 men (seamen and colonizers), five personal servants, six priests to convert the natives, a pack of attack dogs in case of emergency, and fifty horses to carry the men to and from the gold mines. Adelante!

On the way to Hispaniola, Columbus checked new islands for gold, but instead he found cannibals. (He didn't linger.) And pineapples. (Delicious.) Still, he knew that gold lay ahead waiting for him—piles of it perhaps, so he didn't worry.

At ten o'clock on the evening of November 27, Columbus and his men arrived at Hispaniola, expecting a grand reunion with the thirty-nine men left behind. But there were no lights on shore. No sign of life where the fort should be.

When Columbus fired his cannon, there was no answering shot. Going ashore the next morning, Columbus found the fort burned down, the Spaniards dead.

Columbus went to see his friend, the king. What had happened? Tears ran down the king's cheeks. A fierce neighboring tribe had killed the Spaniards, he said. Why? Well, the Spaniards had behaved badly after the admiral left. They had rampaged over the island, stealing from this fierce tribe and mistreating their women. The king said he'd tried to help the Spaniards, but the enemy had been too strong— 3000 men, all angry.

It was clear that the wreck of the *Santa Maria* had not been the miracle that Columbus had supposed, but he didn't admit it. Certainly he didn't give up. He was the kind of man who was always sure that the next day would be better and the next place would have gold.

But nothing went right. Obviously it was not safe to settle where the fort had been, but the new site he picked (Isabela, he called it) was a poor choice—far from fresh water and alive with mosquitoes. The settlers were unhappy and uncooperative. They had come to the Indies to collect gold, not to work in fields, planting crops. Moreover, they resented Columbus, who wasn't even a Spaniard, ordering them about. And they took sick. Sometimes as many as 400 were sick at the same time, in spite of the fact that Columbus had bragged about how healthy his Indies were. The doctor of the expedition said the Spaniards were not used to native food; their own crops had not come up (or not been planted) and the food they had brought with them was running out. The queen's ships would have to be sent back with an order for more supplies.

But send them back without gold? Columbus had promised to return twelve of the ships right away, but he had also promised to load them with gold and spices which the thirty-nine men would have collected in their fort. Columbus managed to scrape up some gold, but not enough even to pay for the expedition. So along with the gold he sent a supply of what he hoped was cinnamon (but wasn't), pepper (that was too strong), sandalwood (that was the wrong color). Also sixty parrots and twenty-six natives. (Three were cannibals.)

When the ships had left, Columbus led a formal expedition inland to Cipangu, or Cybao, as the natives insisted on calling it. They did find some gold—in rocks, in sand along the riverbank, in the possession of natives—but there was no sign of a gold mine. Moreover, Cybao was just like the rest of the island. In no way did it resemble Marco Polo's Cipangu; even Columbus had to admit that. It might be the land that the queen of Sheba had ruled in Bible times, Columbus thought. Like most people of his day, he was far more interested in finding ancient, mysterious places known to exist than in discovering new ones. Any sailor blown off-course might stumble upon a piece of unknown land. What was the glory in that? But he had been wrong too many times lately. He had to be right soon or people might say these weren't even the Indies. Indeed, the Portuguese were already saying it. All Columbus had found, they claimed, was a bunch of islands.

So Columbus left for China. The queen had instructed him to make sure that what he called China (and the natives called Colba or Cuba) was really the mainland and not just another island. Columbus had no doubt about the matter. Of course Colba was a peninsula firmly attached to a continent. But to please the queen, he followed the coastline until he decided it wasn't necessary to go farther. He had found proof enough. In one day, for instance, he had counted 164 new islands. Didn't that sound like Marco Polo's account? And what about the three white men dressed in white tunics that a sailor had seen in the woods? There could be only one explanation: Prester John and two of his followers. And the animal footprints? Big as a lion's, they were. One even looked like the print of a griffon that Sir John Mandeville talked about.

Indeed, Colba *had* to be China, just as this *had* to be the Indies. Columbus had been born to find the Indies. His whole life couldn't be a mistake; God couldn't be wrong. But in case anyone disagreed with him, Christopher Columbus had his entire crew sign an oath, swearing that Colba was part of a continent. The crew was told that if any of them ever denied this, he would have his tongue cut out.

When Columbus returned to Isabela in September 1494, he was sick from nervous exhaustion. What he needed was some good news to cheer him up. What he got was bad news. The mosquitoes were thicker than ever. The people

were in a turmoil—roaming the island, stealing from natives, provoking fights. Some troublemakers had even run off to Spain in stolen ships to spread stories about what a bad governor Columbus was and what a failure his colony had turned out to be.

And what about gold? Ships were waiting in the harbor right now to take gold back to Spain. But there was hardly any gold. What could be sent in its place? There was only one thing that Columbus could think of. Natives. So Columbus had 500 natives captured and placed on shipboard to be taken to Spain and sold as slaves. African explorers were always sending Africans back to Spanish slave markets, Columbus told himself. Besides, the natives were all heathens. It wasn't as if he were selling Christians into slavery. (In fact, there was not a single Christian native in all of Hispaniola. The converting had gone as badly as the gold-mining.)

As soon as the ships had left, Columbus introduced a new system to bring in gold. The settlers were not doing a good job, and unfortunately he had found none of Sir John Mandeville's gold-digging ants. So he turned to the natives again. Every native over fourteen was ordered to turn over one of his small bells filled with gold dust every three months. The bell was not big; still, it was too big. No matter how hard they worked, the natives couldn't find that much gold in the washed-out riverbeds, but when they failed, they were punished. Many ran off to the hills and hid. Some left the island entirely. Between 1494 and 1496 one-third of the native population of Hispaniola was killed, sold, or scared away.

In March 1496, Columbus left for Spain to try to set things right with the king and queen. He had been away for two years and eight months and he had a lot of explaining to do. He couldn't understand what had gone wrong. God must be punishing him. But for what? Perhaps he had been proud and had shown off too much. So as soon as he landed in

Spain, Columbus put on the plain brown robe of a monk. Next to his skin he wore a rough prickly shirt. Then he proceeded to the royal court. Just as before, he had a parade of parrots, natives, and men carrying gold samples and tropical curiosities, but people paid little attention this time. Remember that fellow who found the Indies? they said. Well, he was back again. That man with the beard, in the monk's robe, limping from arthritis—that was the one. They called him "Admiral of the Mosquitoes" now. A man who would sail all the way across the ocean with only some wild-looking birds and mosquito bites to show for it! Sure, there was gold, but was it real? they asked.

The king and queen had, of course, heard the stories, but they weren't quite ready to give up on Columbus. They would send him out again, they said, but this time he was to work harder at converting natives.

So on May 30, 1498, Columbus set sail. This time he was to explore south before going on to Hispaniola. (Europeans generally believed that the farther south one went, the more gold one would find.)

Columbus dedicated this third voyage to the Holy Trinity (the Christian idea of a threefold God) and promised to name the first land he discovered "Trinidad."

Once at sea, Columbus became his old optimistic self, ready to call every piece of good luck a miracle. Indeed, what else but a miracle kept them all from burning to death on the way? In one week of intense heat, casks of wine and water burst, wheat caught fire, bacon and meat was roasted to a crisp, but the men survived.

And what about Trinidad? When the shout went up that land was sighted, there on the horizon was an island with three mountain peaks. *Three* right in a row. Three for the Trinity. That couldn't be an accident, Columbus said.

Across from Trinidad was the continent which we now call South America, but it took Columbus awhile to recognize that it was a continent. He wasn't expecting one and it wasn't easy to fit it into the jumble of geography he had fixed in his head. If this was the Indies (and of course it was) and the

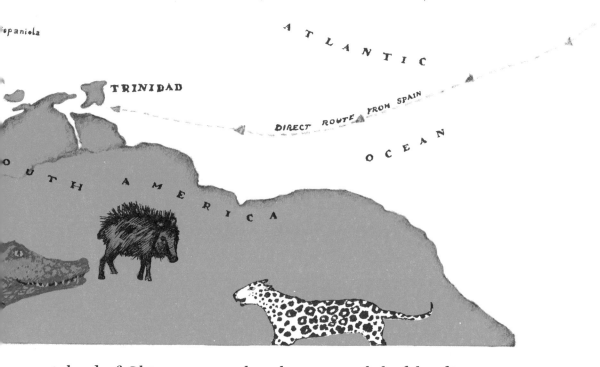

mainland of China was north, what on earth had he discovered? Finally he realized that this must be where the Garden of Eden was. "All men say," he pointed out, "that it's at the end of the Orient and that's where we are." It was impossible for Columbus (or many Europeans at that time) to imagine a whole new world that had never been heard of.

Columbus couldn't stay to look for the Garden. He had supplies to deliver to Hispaniola and as usual trouble was waiting for him. Revolt, corruption, sickness. For two miserable years Columbus tried to govern Spaniards who didn't want to be governed and didn't even want to be where they were. Most particularly they didn't want to be governed by Columbus. Indeed, there were so many complaints about him that the king and queen of Spain decided to find out what was going on.

On August 23, 1500, Francis de Bobadilla, a special representative of the crown, arrived in Hispaniola. The first thing he saw was a gallows on which seven rebel Spaniards were hanging. Bobadilla never tried to find out the right or wrong of it. He simply arrested Columbus then and there. Nor was it enough to jail him. Bobadilla ordered him put in chains, but no one was willing to fasten chains on the

governor-general, the Admiral of the Ocean Sea, and the viceroy of the Indies.

At last Columbus' cook stepped forward. He'd do it, he said. He didn't mind.

So Columbus was put in chains and locked up for two months in Hispaniola. Still in chains, he was sent to Spain. He was offered release, but he refused to have his chains removed until the queen herself gave the order. When they were finally taken off (six weeks after his arrival in Spain), he put the chains on a mantelpiece in his house and asked that they be buried with him. (They weren't.) His chains had become another sign that he'd been specially chosen by God. They were his private cross. For didn't the most faithful always have to suffer the most?

But Columbus didn't suffer quietly. He let everyone know how wronged he'd been. Why, if he'd given the Indies to the Moors, he said, he couldn't have been treated worse! The king and queen reassured him. They hadn't wanted him imprisoned. It had been a mistake and they'd see that Bobadilla was punished. Columbus would receive a share of profits, just as he'd been promised, they said. But they didn't say anything about his going back to the Indies. Columbus was forty-nine years old now, but his hair was white and he was so stiff with arthritis that he seemed older. But not too old, he told himself. He wasn't done with the Indies. There was still another trip in him.

Indeed, it wasn't easy to stay quietly at home in Spain while other men were exploring his Indies, crossing the Ocean Sea that no one had dared to cross until he'd taken the fear out of it. At least five men, some (including Amerigo Vespucci) who had helped Columbus in the past, were leading their own expeditions. Reports came back of strange islands discovered: an island of giants, an island where men ate grass and chewed their cud like cows.

And what was Columbus doing?

Sitting on dry land, twiddling his thumbs.

John Cabot

Vasco da Gama

Farther north, a Genoese named John Cabot, sailing for England, claimed to have reached the Land of the Great Khan. (Actually he went to Newfoundland.) But the man who was causing the greatest sensation was Vasco da Gama, a Portuguese who had succeeded in making the voyage that King John had dreamed of. He had not only sailed around Africa, he had gone on to India, where people were civilized and wore clothes. In 1496 he had returned with spices that were real spices and stories that matched up with Marco Polo's.

Now in 1502 Vasco da Gama was going again. But he was still taking the long way around, Columbus insisted. What's more, Columbus wanted a chance to prove it. All he had to do was explore the western part of his Indies more thoroughly and he'd find a passage that would lead to the other side. From there, it would not be more than a ten-day sail to India. What Vasco da Gama had found was merely an extension of his own Indies.

The king and queen were willing to give Columbus his chance. After all, they didn't like Vasco da Gama's success either. They provided Columbus with four ships, 135 men, an Arabic interpreter, and a letter of introduction to Vasco da Gama in case they should meet in that confusing place both men called the Indies. They also laid down two rules for Columbus. No more slaves. No stopping off in Hispaniola, which now had a new governor. They expected Columbus to find the strait or passageway, proceed to India, and then sail home around the world. If this didn't work out, he could stop off in Hispaniola on the way home. But not on his way out.

Columbus didn't care how many rules there were. No matter what he called himself, no matter that the king and queen had officially restored his privileges, he knew that he wasn't really governor or viceroy of anything now. But at least in March 1502, he was back at sea.

Columbus called this fourth trip his "High Voyage," perhaps his last chance to sail through his beloved Indies, to rejoice in the soft mornings, to lose himself in the night sky. Certainly it seemed as if this time everything would go well. Twenty-one days he had of smooth sailing, right in a row. Twenty-one nights of clear sky, every star in its place. But when feathery clouds raced across the upper sky, when the sea swelled and rolled in from the southeast, Columbus knew that a hurricane was in the making. As it happened, however, he was near a safe harbor.

Hispaniola. Of course, he wasn't supposed to go there. He could obey the queen, sail past, and perhaps drown at sea, but he didn't like that idea. Instead he sent a small boat ashore with a messenger to ask the governor's permission to enter the harbor.

The governor said no. A storm? The governor was sending the queen's fleet of thirty ships back to Spain the next day. That's what *he* thought of the weather. And he didn't want Christopher Columbus coming ashore and making trouble.

Columbus' face turned a fiery red. To be refused shelter in the land he had won for Spain! To have to scurry around in search of a protected cove when his own harbor was right there! Still, when the hurricane struck, Columbus was ready, and when it was over, his four little ships were safe and sound.

But not the queen's fleet. Nineteen ships went down. Five hundred people were drowned, among them Francis de Bobadilla. Indeed, only one of the queen's fleet made it back to Spain and that was the ship carrying Columbus' personal possessions which he'd left behind when he was arrested. The governor and his friends said that Columbus had performed black magic. Columbus said that what had happened was a miracle, pure and simple. And no more than he deserved.

As it turned out, that hurricane was only the beginning of a long siege of stormy weather that pursued Columbus up and down the coast of what we now call Central America. Whatever violence the sky could do, it did. When it rained, Columbus said, it wasn't rain, it was "a deluge." When a storm started, it went on and on—once for twenty-eight days without a letup. "Other tempests have I seen," Columbus wrote in his report, "but none so long or so grim as this." And as if rain, thunder, lightning, and wind were not enough, once a mammoth waterspout appeared, a whirlwindlike column of water that sucked up everything in

its path. In the face of such danger, Columbus felt he had to do something. So with his Bible in his left hand, he raised his sword in his right and traced a cross in the sky. Then he drew a large circle which was meant to enclose his four ships in safety. Pretty soon the waterspout dissolved.

But no matter what he did, Columbus couldn't find a passageway to India. Up and down the coast he sailed, stopping to ask natives the directions to a waterway across the land. As usual the Spaniards used sign language. The

natives nodded, pointed, and made their arms into a circle which the Spaniards understood to mean water. Again and again Columbus followed directions. Again and again he came to water, just as the natives had promised. Every time it was a bay or a lake or a lagoon. Never a passage leading to India. On Christmas night the four ships anchored off Panama, not more than thirty-two miles from the Pacific Ocean, but even if Columbus had known how close he was to the other side, there was no way to reach it with his ships. And if he had reached it, he would, of course, have seen another whole ocean spread before him, although he'd have had no way of knowing how big it was. In any case, by this time Columbus had given up the idea of finding a passage.

Gold. That was what he was after now. North of Panama was a land where he'd found more signs of gold than he'd found in four years in Hispaniola. Indeed, it was here, he said, that King Solomon of Biblical times must have had his gold mines. Columbus spent the spring in this country, building a fort to serve as a trading post, but right from the beginning, the natives had been suspicious and unfriendly. They had a strange custom of turning their backs when they spoke, which, of course, made sign language difficult. But it was clear that they didn't care to talk. On April 6, 1503, a force of 400 natives attacked the Spanish fort and before the fighting was over, twelve Spaniards had been killed.

Columbus, sick with malaria and running a high fever, had been left alone on shipboard. He could hear the battle, but when he cried out to his captains, there was no reply. He must have fainted, he reported later, and while unconscious, he seemed to hear a voice telling him not to be discouraged. Yes, he was an old man, the voice said, but he would still perform brave deeds. Good things still lay in store for him.

This was a comfort to Columbus, but obviously no brave deeds were in order right then. What he and his men had to do now was to escape. Abandoning the fort, King Solomon's mine, and one ship stuck on a sandbar, Columbus set sail for Hispaniola, not even sure he could make it there. His ships had been so eaten by shipworms that they were falling apart, and, indeed, another ship had to be abandoned within a few

days. For two months the two remaining ships stumbled through the water while the men pumped and bailed, but on June 25, when they reached the island of Jamaica, the ships could stay afloat no longer. The men ran them ashore and beached them close together, for this was where they would live. For how long, no one knew. They were marooned.

Columbus was stranded on Jamaica for one year and five days. He spent most of that time trying to control his men (half of them mutinied), trying to keep peace with the natives (who supplied them with food), and feeling sorry for himself.

At first he had hoped for a quick rescue. Diego Mendez, a gentleman volunteer, had left in a native canoe in July for Hispaniola to bring help. But as summer turned into winter and winter into spring, Columbus decided that Diego had drowned on the way. What else could he think? He had no way of knowing that Diego had reached Hispaniola safely but that the governor was in no hurry to help Christopher Columbus. He had no ship large enough that he could spare, he said, nor did he send one until June 1504.

Columbus was fifty-three years old now, in poor health, and impatient to see the queen. He still had brave deeds to perform, he wanted to tell her. But there were delays in Hispaniola. There was bad weather at sea. Columbus did not reach Spain until November 7, 1504. And he never did see Queen Isabella. She died on November 26, three weeks after his arrival.

His dream of brave deeds faded with the queen's death. It was she who had supported him in the past, not the king, who had never shown much faith in him. Moreover, Columbus was in no condition now for brave deeds. Many days he was too crippled with arthritis even to get out of bed, so he concentrated instead on trying to collect the rewards he felt were his due. He had become a wealthy man over the years, receiving a portion of profits from the Indies, but it was not as large a portion as had been agreed upon, he insisted. He wanted his original contract with the king and queen fulfilled. Only in this way, he believed, would his success be officially acknowledged. He spent much of his time peti-

tioning the king and complaining. He and his friend Amerigo Vespucci would get together and deplore the fate of explorers. How unappreciated they were! How neglected!

Certainly Columbus had performed brave deeds, but not even he could appreciate the extent of his achievement. Until the day he died, May 20, 1506, he refused to revise his geography although by this time others were questioning it. A pilot on Columbus' second voyage drew a map showing Colba as an island, but Columbus insisted to the end that it was China. He had gone to find the Indies, he said, and he'd found them.

After his death, explorers picked up where Columbus left off, and a true picture of the world slowly began to emerge. In 1513 Balboa crossed those few miles at Panama and claimed the Pacific Ocean for Spain. In 1520, near the tip of South America, Ferdinand Magellan found the waterway that Columbus had failed to find on his fourth voyage. Although Magellan did not survive his expedition, one of his original five ships arrived in Spain in 1522, having actually completed the trip around the world that Columbus had planned. When Magellan's men told their story, it was obvious that the world was much bigger than anyone supposed. Whereas Columbus had figured it was 2400 miles from the Canary Islands to Japan, it was actually 10,000. Indeed, Columbus' world was 25% smaller than the real world, and there was 55% more water in the world than he had figured. With such information, it became increasingly clear that all that land between Europe and Asia must be a New World, previously unknown to Europeans.

Columbus would have been upset to hear this news. He was convinced that he knew the secrets of the world, and he didn't like to be wrong. The last thing that he had wanted to do was to discover a New World.

NOTES

10. Columbus was born sometime between August 25 and October 31, but it was the custom then to celebrate the feast day of a person's patron saint rather than his own birthday. St. Christopher's feast day is June 25.

    Christopher had three younger brothers and a younger sister. His brother Bartholomew worked with him in the map store in Portugal. In 1494 he joined Christopher in Hispaniola and took an active part in the government. Christopher's youngest brother, Diego, accompanied him on his second and third voyages.

    The Turks were Mohammedans—followers of the prophet Mohammed (as Christians are followers of Christ). Mohammedans in the Mid-East held the Holy City of Jerusalem, which for centuries the Christians had been trying to recapture. In 1453 the Turks captured Constantinople, where the trade routes to the East met. Now they were able to control overland traffic.

14. A nautical (or sea) mile is approximately 800 feet longer than a land mile. Marco Polo really did have fabulous experiences in China, but he never went to Japan and his description is inaccurate and based on hearsay.

17. While Columbus was in Spain, he met Beatriz Enriquez de

77

Haraña, the daughter of a peasant. Since Columbus was dealing with royalty, he did not think it suitable to marry Beatriz, yet he remained devoted to her throughout his life. Their son, Ferdinand, was born in 1488. In 1494 both of Christopher's sons, Diego and Ferdinand, became pages at the Spanish court. Ferdinand went with his father on his last voyage and later wrote a biography of him.

24. The Sargasso Sea, east of the West Indies, is noted for the abundance of gulfweed on its surface.

26. Columbus' reckoning of distance was not accurate on this trip. The figures he gave the sailors happened to be closer to the true distance than the record he kept for himself.

31. The natives Columbus saw throughout his travels were usually naked, although on some islands they wore loincloths. On his last voyage he found natives who also wore bandanas.

33. When the Spaniards asked questions, the natives probably nodded or said just what they thought the Spaniards wanted to hear. Of course there were no dog-headed or other strange-looking people in the Indies. Sir John Mandeville told sensational and untrue stories because he wanted his book to be read.

40. Actually this "king" was a head chief, or cacique, who ruled northwestern Haiti.

50. The Spaniards used these dogs with great success in fighting natives. One dog, they said, was equal to eight men. The natives were also terrified of horses. When they saw a man on horseback, they thought it was all one animal.

56. Before leaving Isabela, Columbus ordered that a new city be built on a more suitable site to replace the old one. The new city, begun in 1496 or 1497, was called Santo Domingo. It was here that Columbus was denied the right to land during the hurricane. The island that Columbus called Hispaniola is now divided into two countries: Haiti in the west, the Dominican Republic in the east. Columbus dressed in a monk's robe for the rest of his life.

60. Columbus' enemies represented him as a tyrant, but even his friends agreed that Columbus was an indiscreet, tactless, and unsuccessful governor. The Spaniards whom Bobadilla saw hanging, however, were indeed guilty of leading a rebellion.

75. Columbus' "Garden of Eden" continent was given the name "America" in 1507, just a year after his death. A French geographer had read an account of Amerigo Vespucci's visit to this continent. This account, however, was falsely dated 1497, a year before Columbus' visit, instead of 1499 when it actually took place. So the geographer gave Vespucci the credit for the discovery and wrote "America" on the new map he was making.

76. When one speaks of the "discovery" of America, one is taking the European point of view, from which this story is told. Strictly speaking, of course, native Americans discovered the New World thousands of years before. Betweentimes, the Vikings came, perhaps the Phoenicians, perhaps sailors from other countries. These were separate trips and had no lasting effect on history. Columbus' voyages, however, set off a wave of exploration that changed the world forever. He deliberately crossed an ocean that few people thought could be crossed. And luckily he was a magnificent seaman.

Index